PB

Spotlight on
South Africa

Bobbie Kalman

🌳 Crabtree Publishing Company

www.crabtreebooks.com

Spotlight On My Country

Created by Bobbie Kalman

For Marc and Joanna Crabtree,
who spent their honeymoon in South Africa.
Lots of love to you both!

**Author and
Editor-in-Chief**
Bobbie Kalman

Editors
Kathy Middleton
Crystal Sikkens

Fact editors
Marcella Haanstra
Enlynne Paterson

Design
Bobbie Kalman
Katherine Berti
Samantha Crabtree (cover)

Photo research
Bobbie Kalman

**Print and production coordinator
and prepress technician**
Katherine Berti

Photographs
Associated Press: page 25 (top
    and bottom)
iStockphoto: pages 16, 31 (top left)
Keystone Press: © Matthew Childs/
    Zumapress.com: page 29 (top right)
Photos.com: pages 9 (top left), 23
    (bottom left)
Other images by Shutterstock

Library and Archives Canada Cataloguing in Publication

Kalman, Bobbie, 1947-
    Spotlight on South Africa / Bobbie Kalman.

(Spotlight on my country)
Includes index.
Issued also in electronic format.
ISBN 978-0-7787-3464-2 (bound).--ISBN 978-0-7787-3490-1 (pbk.)

    1. South Africa--Juvenile literature. I. Title. II. Series: Spotlight
on my country

DT1719.K34 2011   j968   C2011-900003-2

Library of Congress Cataloging-in-Publication Data

Kalman, Bobbie.
 Spotlight on South Africa / Bobbie Kalman.
   p. cm. -- (Spotlight on my country)
 Includes index.
 ISBN 978-0-7787-3490-1 (pbk. : alk. paper) -- ISBN 978-0-7787-3464-2
(reinforced library binding : alk. paper) -- ISBN 978-1-4271-9687-3
(electronic (pdf)
 1. South Africa--Juvenile literature. I. Title. II. Series: Spotlight on my
country.

DT1719.K35 2011
968--dc22
                                        2010051454

Crabtree Publishing Company

www.crabtreebooks.com   1-800-387-7650

Printed in the U.S.A./022011/CJ20101228

Published in Canada
Crabtree Publishing
616 Welland Ave.
St. Catharines, Ontario
L2M 5V6

Published in the United States
Crabtree Publishing
PMB 59051
350 Fifth Avenue, 59th Floor
New York, New York 10118

Published in the United Kingdom
Crabtree Publishing
Maritime House
Basin Road North, Hove
BN41 1WR

Published in Australia
Crabtree Publishing
386 Mt. Alexander Rd.
Ascot Vale (Melbourne)
VIC 3032

Contents

Where is South Africa?

South Africa is a **country** in the southern part of Africa. A country is an area of land on which people live. It has **borders** that separate it from other countries. South Africa shares its borders with Namibia, Botswana, Zimbabwe, Mozambique, and Swaziland. One country, Lesotho, is completely inside South Africa, but it is not part of the country. South Africa is divided into nine provinces. Find the provinces and countries on the map below.

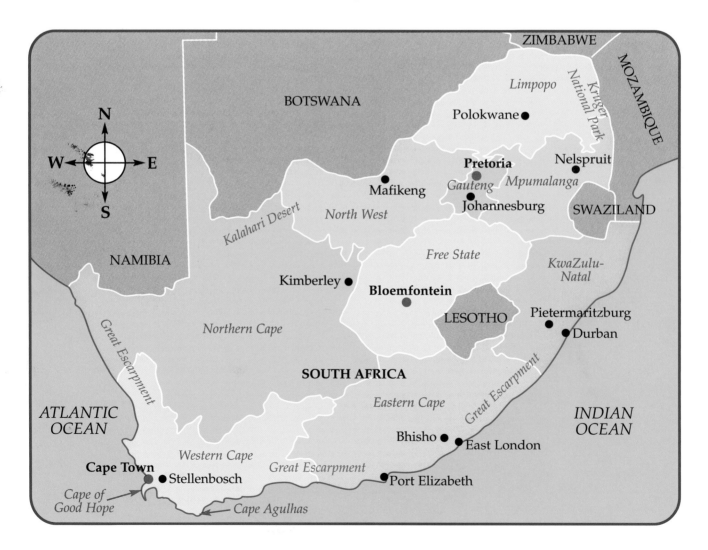

Seven continents and five oceans

South Africa is part of the **continent** of Africa. A continent is a huge area of land. The other continents are North America, South America, Europe, Asia, Antarctica, and Australia/Oceania. The seven continents are shown on the world map below. Earth's five oceans flow around the continents. Two oceans touch South Africa. Which oceans are they?

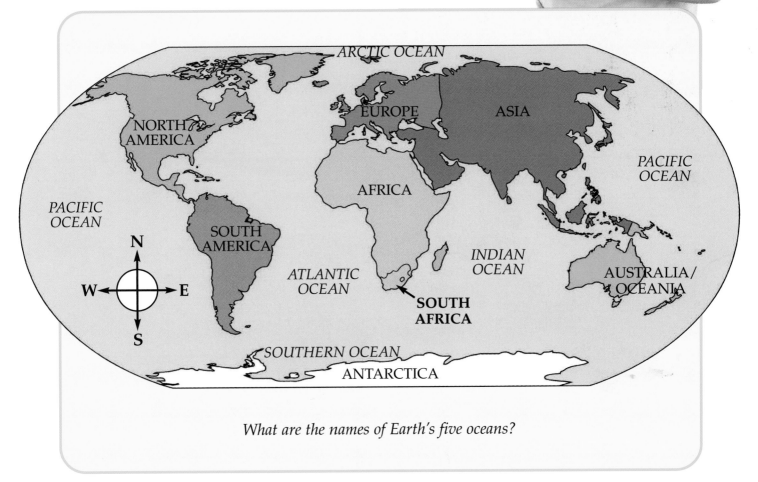

What are the names of Earth's five oceans?

Two oceans

South Africa lies at the southern tip of the African continent. Water surrounds the country on three sides. Two oceans come together at the southern part of the country. They are the Atlantic Ocean and the Indian Ocean. The Cape of Good Hope is a narrow piece of rocky land that juts out into the ocean. The people who live near it believe that the two oceans meet at this famous cape.

Cape Agulhas is the most southern point of Africa and is officially recognized as the place where the Atlantic and Indian oceans meet.

Cape Town is on the Atlantic Ocean about 31 miles (50 km) north of the Cape of Good Hope. It is South Africa's oldest city and second-largest city in population.

South Africa's people

The **population** of South Africa is about 50 million people. Population is the number of people who live in a country. South Africa is known as the "Rainbow Nation" because the people who live there have come from many different backgrounds. They speak eleven different languages: English, Afrikaans, *isiXhosa*, *isiZulu*, *isiNdebele*, *Sepedi*, *Sesotho*, *siSwati*, *Xitsonga*, *Setswana*, and *Tshivenda*. Some people speak three or more languages. Below is a chart of some words and phrases in five different South African languages. Try saying some of these words and greetings.

English	Afrikaans	*isiXhosa*	*Tshivenda*	*isiZulu*
Hello	Hallo	Molo	Nda	Sakubona
Good morning	Goeiemore	Molo	Ndi matsheloni	Sakubona
How are you?	Hoe gaan dit?	Unjani?	No vuwa hani?	Unjani?
I am fine.	Dit gaan goed	Ndiphilile	Ndi hone	Ngiyaphila
Good night	Goeienag	Rhonanai	Ndi madekwana	Salakahle
Goodbye	Tot siens	Hamba kakuhle	Salani zwavhudi	Hambakah
Yes	Ja	Ewe	Ee	Yebo
No	Nee	Xha	Hai	Cha
Please	Asseblief	Ndicela	Ndihumbela	Ngiyacela
Thank you	Dankie	Ndiyabonga	Ndolivhuwo	Ngiyabong

These girls are Afrikaners. Their **ancestors** came from the Netherlands many years ago. They speak Afrikaans.

The Ndebele people live in northeast South Africa, near the capital city of Pretoria. They speak isiNdebele.

The Zulu make up the largest South African ethnic group—about ten to eleven million people. They live mainly in the KwaZulu-Natal province. Their language is isiZulu. The name Zulu means "people of heaven."

The young woman holding a South African flag is Indian. Most Indians came to South Africa in the late 1800s to work on sugar **plantations**, or large farms. Indian South Africans speak mainly English.

Big cities

More than half of the people in South Africa live in cities. There are three capital cities, and each one controls a different part of the government. Pretoria is the national capital city and is the **administrative** center. Cape Town is the **legislative** capital and is the country's oldest and largest city in land area. Bloemfontein, which means "fountain of flowers," is the **judicial** capital. Another city, Johannesburg, has the biggest population and is the country's business center. Durban is the third-largest city. It is on the Indian Ocean.

Pretoria is a beautiful city with tall buildings and lovely parks.

Durban is on the Indian Ocean. It has wonderful weather and beautiful beaches. Many Indian South Africans live in this city. Long ago, they sailed across the Indian Ocean from India to work in South Africa.

Johannesburg is South Africa's biggest city in population. The township of Soweto is part of Johannesburg (see page 24).

Life in the country

People sell crafts such as carved statues.

In the past, most South Africans lived in villages in the countryside. A village could have as few as 50 people or as many as several hundred. People in the villages grew **crops**, such as corn, yams, and **millet**, for food. They worked hard looking after **livestock**, or farm animals. Today, life in the villages is still hard. People may live far from stores, schools, and hospitals. Many villagers do not have water in their homes and must walk long distances to get it. To make money, some people work on large farms owned by Afrikaners. Others make extra money selling crafts at markets.

Some South African villages have only a few houses.

This farm belongs to an Afrikaner.
Many people from nearby villages work on this farm.

The older children in villages help look after the younger ones.

Many villages do not have water. People must walk a long way to get it.

South Africa's land

South Africa is a beautiful country with spectacular mountains, beautiful beaches, and sweeping desert sands. Most of the countryside is covered by grassland, which is called **veld**. Much of South Africa's land is Highveld. Highveld is made up of higher areas with flat or gently rolling hills and cool weather. Lower areas are known as Lowveld. These areas are much hotter. A long ridge of mountains, called the Great Escarpment, separates the coast from the interior land.

Drakensberg, or Dragon Mountains, are part of the escarpment. This picture shows Blyde River Canyon in Drakensberg. A canyon is a deep area, often containing a river. Hippos, apes, monkeys, crocodiles, antelopes, and fish live in this canyon.

The Kalahari Desert is in the northwestern part of South Africa. Very little rain falls in deserts, so the land is dry. This cape fox looks for mice, insects, and spiders to eat in the desert. It also eats plants.

The mountain in this picture is called Table Mountain because it is flat like a table. The long cloud that forms above the mountain is called its "tablecloth." Table Mountain is near Cape Town. Each spring after it rains, many fields in South Africa are covered with colorful wild flowers like these.

15

Super animals!

South Africa is home to many of the most fascinating animals on Earth! In the oceans around South Africa, you might see whales, dolphins, and big sharks. On land, you might meet a huge elephant, or its much smaller relative, the rock hyrax. You might even spot a cheetah running across a grassy veld. Look up! Can you see the tallest animal on Earth eating the leaves of an acacia tree? What is this animal called?

This rock hyrax has found a feast of spring flowers to eat.

The black mamba, the world's longest and most poisonous snake, lives in South Africa.

Great white sharks swim in the oceans around South Africa. In a lifetime, a shark can have 50,000 teeth! The teeth break, fall out, and are constantly replaced.

The cheetah, shown above, is the fastest land animal on Earth! Wild cats, such as cheetahs, leopards, and lions, live in South Africa.

Big and tall

Two of the biggest land animals in South Africa are the elephant and the giraffe. The elephant is the largest and heaviest. Did you guess that the giraffe is the tallest?

Kruger National Park

Paul Kruger, a president of South Africa, wanted to protect wild animals from being hunted. His statue stands at the park.

About 100 years ago, many of South Africa's animals were **endangered**, or in danger of disappearing from Earth. People cut down forests and hunted animals, such as lions, elephants, and leopards. To protect these animals, the government set up **preserves**, or huge parks, where animals would be safe. The largest is Kruger National Park, where the animals roam free.

A female lion and a leopard tortoise have a drink at a water hole in Kruger Park.

Unusual living things

In this park, there are more than 147 **species**, or types, of mammals, 114 species of reptiles, 507 species of birds, and 50 species of fish. There are also many species of trees, flowers, and grasses that do not grow in other places.

(above) Baobab trees can live for more than a thousand years. They are called "upside-down trees" because their branches look like roots.

(left) The protea is South Africa's national flower. This large flower can be 12 inches (30 cm) across.

This male kudu is standing among some unusual plants in Kruger Park.

Farming and fishing

South Africa's warm temperatures are perfect for growing different crops and raising livestock, or farm animals. In most parts of South Africa, livestock can **graze**, or feed, on the short grasses that grow in the fields. Cows are raised for milk and meat, and sheep and goats are raised for their wool. Ostriches are raised for their meat and skin. Their skin is made into leather. Fruits such as bananas, oranges, grapes, apples, and mangoes are grown on huge farms.

*Grapes are grown in large **vineyards** all around Cape Town and along the southern coasts. Some of the grapes are sold fresh, and some are dried and sold as raisins. Most of the grapes are used to make wine. Many vineyards are in the Stellenbosch area, shown above. Stellenbosch is near Cape Town.*

At some ostrich farms, visitors can eat ostrich steaks, watch ostrich races, or ride ostriches. This ostrich has laid some eggs.

The waters around South Africa are great places for fishing and for catching lobsters. Lobsters are trapped in cages like these.

Life long ago

This woman is a descendant of the San, one of the first peoples in South Africa.

This old house was built by an Afrikaner settler.

The first people to come to South Africa from other parts of Africa were the San and Khoikhoi. The San moved from place to place, hunting animals and gathering plants for food. About 1,500 years ago, Bantu-speaking peoples from northern Africa came with their cattle and set up farms and villages. South Africans, such as the Zulu, Sotho, Tswana, Ndebele, and Xhosa, are **descendants** of these peoples.

Europeans settle in South Africa

About 500 years ago, people from Europe sailed to and from Asia for spices. On their way, they stopped at the Cape of Good Hope to get fresh food and water. In 1652, 90 Dutch **settlers** came to live in the Cape. The settlers were called Boers, which means "farmers" in the Dutch language. Settlers also came from France and Germany. All these people became known as Afrikaners.

The British take over

In the early 1800s, the British took control of Cape Town to prevent France from invading. Several thousand English people settled there. Some became farmers, who brought workers from India. Others set up businesses and settled along the coast in cities such as East London, Durban, and Port Elizabeth.

The Afrikaners move

The Afrikaners were not happy under British rule. In the 1830s, several thousand Boers gave up their land and made a difficult trip inland to claim new farmland. They fought the Zulus and other South African peoples, took over their lands, and forced them to work on their farms.

The Boer War

In the late 1800s, the British tried to take over the areas where Afrikaners had built their farms because diamonds and gold were found on the land. The Boer War broke out between the British and the Afrikaners. Thousands of people died, including many black South Africans. The British forced Afrikaner women and children to live in camps, such as the one on the left. Many people died in these camps. In 1902, the Afrikaners **surrendered**, and South Africa became part of the British Empire.

Separate lives

In 1910, South Africa became its own country, called the Union of South Africa. Only people with white skin could vote in the elections, and black people had very few rights. Life got even harder for black Africans after 1948, when the government started **apartheid**. Apartheid means "separateness" in the Afrikaans language. Apartheid divided people into four groups: Whites, Indians, Coloreds, and Blacks. Each group had different rights. People were told where they could live, what kind of jobs they could do, and whom they could marry. The British and Afrikaners were the Whites and had the most rights. The Blacks had the fewest rights.

*Soweto is just outside Johannesburg. It is a crowded area where South Africans with black skin were forced to live during apartheid. Other crowded areas like this were called **shantytowns**.*

The heroes of apartheid

Thousands of people lost their lives fighting to end apartheid. Others spent years in prison for trying to lead people to freedom.

Nelson Mandela

Nelson Mandela was one of the greatest fighters for equality. He organized groups against apartheid and held protests. He was put in prison for 27 years for his role against apartheid. In 1990, he was released from prison by President de Klerk. In 1994, he became South Africa's president.

Nelson Mandela is a hero to South Africans and to people all over the world.

Mandela spent most of his 27 years in prison in these buildings on Robben Island.

Desmond Tutu

Desmond Tutu was an Anglican **archbishop** who wanted to end apartheid without violence. Nelson Mandela, President de Klerk, and Desmond Tutu were given **Nobel Peace Prizes** for their roles in ending apartheid.

Archbishop Tutu inspired people around the world to pressure the government to end apartheid.

25

What is culture?

South Africa has many **cultures**. Culture is the beliefs, customs, and ways of life that a group of people shares. Ways of life include the way people dress, the foods they eat, the crafts they create, and the sports and games they play. People also create art, music, and dances to **express**, or show, their cultures. The images on these pages show some of the arts, crafts, music, dances, and foods that are traditional parts of South Africa's different cultures.

The Ndebele people paint the walls of their homes in brightly colored patterns.

(above) The San people of long ago made paintings of their lives on the walls of caves.

(right) This traditional South African meal includes meat, potatoes, rice, and vegetables.

(below) These women are performing a Zulu dance.

Drums and shakers are used in African music.

Having a ball!

vuvuzela

Playing the vuvuzela during soccer games has become a tradition among South African fans. The horn is made to resemble a kudu horn (see page 19). Vuvuzela horns sound similar to bees buzzing.

The most popular sport in South Africa is soccer, known there as football. The British first brought the game to the country. Soccer quickly became popular with Africans because it was fun, exciting, and cost nothing to play. Players could make their own balls from rags, paper, plastic bags, and other scraps wrapped tightly together with tape. Under apartheid, black and white players were not allowed to play together. Black players were not even allowed to meet in groups because the government feared they would plan protests against apartheid.

World Cup games in 2010

South Africa was the proud host of the 2010 World Cup of soccer. The games were attended by over three million people. Teams from 32 countries competed in the month-long games, which were held in ten stadiums in nine cities around the country. Two of the stadiums were in Johannesburg.

Siphiwe Tshabalala, number 8 on South Africa's national team, Bafana Bafana, scored the first goal of the games. That goal made him the country's hero.

Nelson Mandela and Archbishop Desmond Tutu celebrated the "Rainbow Nation" of South Africa. Tutu was at the World Cup Kick-off Concert, above, at the Orlando Stadium in Soweto. Mandela was at the closing ceremonies.

(right) People from all over the world came to South Africa to watch the games and wave the flags of their countries. The World Cup games showed South Africa as a strong and confident nation. Soccer in South Africa is a symbol of what is possible when people have fun together.

Into the future

Apartheid is no longer a law in South Africa, but it will take time before people feel truly equal. To make sure that people can get better jobs, the government has made it **illegal**, or against the law, to refuse a job to anyone based on their race, religion, or gender. Many black people are now earning the same as white people for doing the same jobs. As well, new homes are being built to replace the shantytowns. The government is also allowing farmers to borrow money so they can raise better animals and buy better seeds for crops.

Some people have better jobs with more pay, but many are still living in shantytowns.

Children of all backgrounds can now be friends.

Children are proud of their Rainbow Nation.

More young people are getting a better education.

Soccer showed the world the new South Africa.

People are getting better health care.

31

Glossary

Note: Some boldfaced words are defined where they appear in the book.

administrative Relating to running a government

ancestor A family member from long ago

apartheid Separation based on skin color

archbishop A bishop with a high rank in a Roman Catholic, Episcopal, Orthodox, Anglican, or other Christian church

border An imaginary line separating two countries or places

country An area of land that has borders and a government

crops Plants grown for food

culture The way of life of a group of people

descendant Someone who is related to a person who lived before them

endangered Describing a living thing that is in danger of dying out

illegal Something that is against the law

judicial Relating to courts that enforce laws

legislative The part of government that makes laws

millet A cereal grain grown for food

Noble Peace Prize A prize awarded to someone for his or her work in promoting world peace

population The number of people or animals in a certain place

preserve A natural area set aside by a country's government to protect the plants and animals living there

settlers People who make new homes in places where few other people live

shantytown A crowded area of a city or town where people live in poorly built homes

species A group of closely related living things that can make babies together

surrender To give up fighting an enemy

veld A flat grassland in Africa

vineyard A field where grapes grow

Index